Life's Poetry

ISBN-13:
978-1523969678

ISBN-10:
1523969679

I0428837

This work is a compilation of poems written by Dean R. Giles. Most of them were written as my ruminations about life, the funny and miraculous situations and observations that make up every-day living..

If you enjoy these poems, please leave a review on Amazon.

(http://amzn.to/1QTnDnI)

Reviews help so much. Thank you in advance.

I also have a number of fiction and non-fiction books published. You can see them at:

Http://AustinsGift.com.

Please send me an email, I love hearing from readers. dean@austinsgift.com

Dean R. Giles

Table of Contents

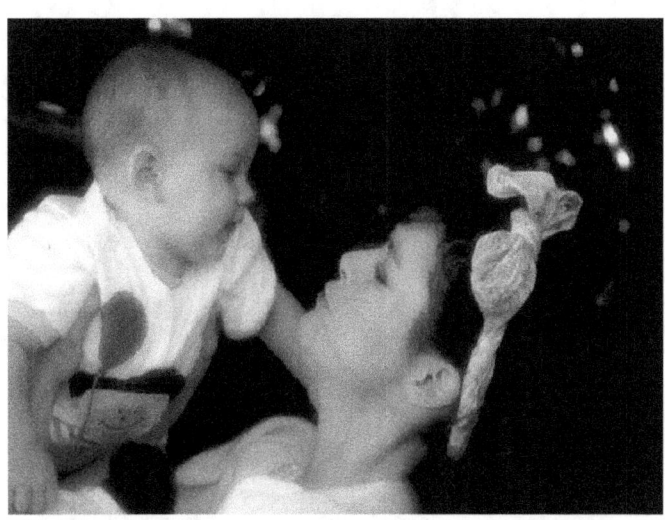

The Miracle of Mothers

There is no comfort like a mother's touch,
It calms all anxious fears and such.
It heals hurt feeling of the day,
And makes the "owies" go away.

There is no soothing like a mother's lips,
Sweetest songs dance from their tips.
And they can press upon a forehead dear,
A kiss of comfort, love, and cheer.

There is no pillow like a mother's breast,
Where her child's sleepy head can rest.
Where neatly gathered on her lap,
Her little child can safely nap.

There is no shelter like a mother's love,
      To shield her child from the storms above.
To protect her child from the cold outside,
      To teach compassion, care, and pride.

There is no miracle in God's great earth,
      That compares to the one that does give birth,
And guides her child through great and small,
      When God made mothers, he out did them all.

Awesome

If you asked me to define "awesome,"
      I'd say, "that's easy," it's "my dad."
He's the one who stood beside me,
      Through the good times and the bad.

Dad is someone who will listen,
      He never seems too busy to care,
His advice comes with a story,
      Or in a thought that he will share.

My dad has a love for people,
      His heart is good and kind.
In his little deeds for others,
      True compassion you will find.

His children are his treasure,
        He helps them know they have true worth.
He put time into his every child,
        From the day of each child's birth.

Family games and family outings,
        Were the highlights of the day.
From family work on family projects,
        Dad would teach us in his way.

He made me feel that I was needed,
        He knew what I could be.
He gave me projects that seemed important,
        Then let me just be me!

If I failed or if I succeeded,
        Neither mattered in the end.
He'd say he's proud to be my father,
        And was blessed to be my friend.

Now, he's not rich nor famous,
        Not anything like that.
He just takes the time for family,
        He proudly wears a Father's hat.

I got a call from my daddy,
        Sometime earlier this year.
He said he just became a great-grandpa,
        I could hear him smile from ear to ear.

So when I hear of other fathers,
        Who are outrageous, cool, or rad...
I just know they couldn't hold a candle,
        To my totally awesome dad.

Brenda

There's a name that stirs the willows,
      And is light upon the air.
In my mind it's always present,
      And it's often in my prayer.

That name is very dear to me,
      Of my life it's now a part.
It calms my troubled moments,
      And brings peace into my heart.

That name is very lovely,
        It's more than just a word.
The person that it represents,
        Is an example to the world.

Oh, Brenda, you inspire me,
        More than simple words can say,
You always show your kindness,
        And brighten up my day.

You always think of others,
        You're unselfish with your time.
You're there when your family needs you,
        And to other's faults you're blind.

You have a love of children,
        And I know they love you too.
I can see it in their eyes,
        Every time they speak of you.

And one more thing I have to say,
        You are smiling all the time.
And in this world of nickels,
        To me you are a dime.

You Brighten Up My Life

You brighten up my life,
  Like blooming flowers in springtime.

Your bubbling laughter is the well-spring

that feeds my soul.
Your love is so deep that it gives my life's roots the
strength to bloom brightly,
Making life with you a stroll through
the most beautiful garden.

A Mother's Gifts

A mothers kiss is soft enough to sooth most any pain,
A peck, soft words, and soon, her child's on his feet again.

A mother's hug is firm enough to comfort any fear,
Her child is filled with confidence just feeling she is near.

A mother's praise is reward enough to face the hardest task.
Her words ring true within his heart, he'll do anything she'll ask.

A mother's hope is bright enough to show a child the way,
Because he saw it in her eyes, he will not turn astray.

A mother's patience is true enough to see where others are blind,
Her unceasing work can unlock in him the best her child can find.

A mother's love is deep enough to give up all she wanted to be,
Sacrificing everything—to be a mother and have a family.

The End of Summer

The falling sand in an hourglass measures the quietly-
fleeting time,
The constant heartbeat of a grandfather clock is
interrupted by a chime.

The warmth of lazy summer days gives way to the cool
evenings of fall.
And a melancholy sigh escapes my lips as fondly I recall.

The constant heat of summer sun, the refreshing taste of
lemonade,
Burning feet on cement walks, the pleasure of resting in
shade.

A cold splash of water from a cup, a frigid stream coming
from the hose,
Perhaps I started that water fight, maybe not, who really
knows?

A frozen popsicle on a stick, coloring my tongue and hand,
Splashing about in a pool, and building castles in the sand.

Laying still in cool grass, watching the clouds go dancing by,
Sleeping out in the open air and counting stars up in the sky.

Betrayed again by the constant drumming of a simple clock on the wall,
Who sweeps away the days of summer and nonchalantly ushers in the fall.

But unknowingly and unfailingly, the fall plants the seeds of it's own demise,
The return of summer is one day closer with each and every new sunrise.

Autumn

There's a nip to the morning air,
It turns my breath to haze.
The cold breeze ruffles my hair,
As autumn meets my gaze.

The litter of withered leaves,
Blanket the stone hard ground.
Mocking the naked trees,

With a rustling and crackly sound.

Patches of yellowing lawn,
Fringed white with glistening frost,
Make a stunning quilt at dawn,
Which is warmed by the sun and lost.

The colors of fall surround me,
Yellow, and red, and brown.
The world is shedding its glory,
But awaiting a white winter crown.

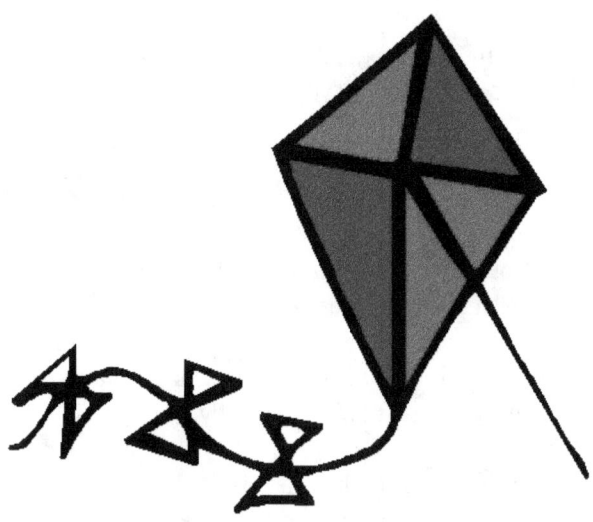

Springtime Awakening

The warm spring breeze awakened it from its winter
sleep.
A fragrant waft of air made it shimmer slightly in its keep.

The sounds of birds chirping called it softly from outside
the door,
It silently called back, and the children noticed it in its
dusty store.

Daddy, daddy, come here they said,
Look on the shelf, get that thing that is red.

I took it down from the shelf, and shook off the dust,
It looked fragile, I was worried, afraid it would bust.

As I stepped from the garage, it tugged on the string,
Step back all, I cried, I'll show you something.

Watch the master at work, and slowly you'll learn,
How to handle this bird, then you'll get your turn.

With the first burst of air, it shot up with a bound,
Then turned with a jerk, and dove straight to the ground.

The children howled with laughter, one said with a sigh,
Even daddy-the-great couldn't make it fly.

Give me that thing, said the littlest one,
Then off to the dirt hill he went on the run.

From the top of the mound, he gave it a toss,
The look on his face said he'd show it who's boss.

At first it bobbled weakly, then started to rise,
Then shot up very quickly into the skies.

The children were awed, one said give it some slack,
No, said another, please make it come back!

I want to try it, now give it to me,
I want a turn, hey, watch out for the tree.

Go to the left, no go to the right,
Stay on top of the hill, don't let it go out of sight!

The little one looked at each want to be flier,
But kept letting out string and sent it up higher.

The natives got restless, the whining got sore,
Finally I thought I just can't take any more.

We went back to the house and ransacked the place,
We searched through every nook, cranny, and space.

We gathered all the spare kite pieces and string that there was.
We taped and patched together four more kites in a buzz.

Out to the dirt hills, and up in the air,
The kites flew with grace as if they hadn't a care.

Some dove to and fro, sometimes hitting the ground,
Other crossed strings and wound round and round.

But the night fell too soon, and each kite was reeled in,
And the children all trudged to the house with a grin.

Their kites now stored safely, but with a hint of unease,
Just waiting to be woken by the next springtime breeze.

Race Against The Sun

Over the mountains came the sun,
Rays of sunlight, on the run,
Calm and quiet, but not still,
Reflecting off my window sill.

By coincidence or fickle fate,
The mocking light did try to bait,
And sent a challenge with a twist,
By lighting up my to-do list.

Aha! I thought, a test indeed.
I'll show that sun my blazing speed.
He has but to make his daily trek,
And I, each task off my list must check.

To the window, with horror, I did dart,
To see that he already had a head start.
Quick, to item number one,
I jumped right to it on the run.

I worked as hard and as fast as I could,
My legs moved as swiftly as they would.
But, I realized my kids just would not last,
Unless they were fed a little breakfast.

So, I stopped my work, and got us something to eat.
Sometimes even simple meals are a big feat.
Soon breakfast was done, and all put away,
The children were cleaned up and starting to play.

I looked at my list, and heaved a big sigh.
Working alone this just will not fly.
Nathan, I said, please go mow the lawn.
Check one off my list, soon each one will be gone.

Jenny, could you vacuum the floor?
Austin, clean the crayon off of this door.
Brenda, which task on this list fits your taste?
Quickly all, now, we have no time to waste.

I then picked the quickest tasks I could find,
Hoping the others wouldn't notice or mind.
Then finally the big tasks, my attention did need,
And so to the garden I trotted to weed.

The heat of the afternoon beat on my back,
The force of the hoe weakened with each passing whack.
That's cheating, I yelled at the blazing sun!
He glared hotly back as if I were spoiling his fun.

All right, I said, let's go get cleaned up.
We'll stop at McDonalds for an on-the-way sup.
Then we'll find the park at the end of the lane,
We'll have some fun just to keep ourselves sane.

At last I sat on the bench for some rest,
And I pulled out my list—totally un-stressed.
I checked off a few, then added some more.
I just can't believe each have-to-do chore…

I chuckled at the setting sun, and I said,
Don't look so cocky you big ball of red.
I concede today, but tomorrow will come.
Don't think for a minute that you've totally won!

Halloween

I hear the gentle wind through the leafless trees,
And feel the nip of a cold October breeze.
The crispness of the full-moon-lit night,
Accentuates the strange and eerie sight.

The laughing jack-o-lantern's flaming eyes,
Leer at hurried, haunting passer-bys.

Startling creatures peer through windows and from doors,
Creepy vistas cover yards and houses by the scores.

Giggling apparitions stalk the porch-lamp-lit streets,
Bags in hand accumulating vast assorted treats.
Three little ghouls, at my door I chance to meet,
A witch, a wolf, a pirate, chanting, trick or treat!

The bounty they seek after are sugar-coated gems,
I offer them Butterfingers, Mounds, and M&Ms.
Oh, what sweet anguish fills the heart in each little chest,
To choose only one, then politely leave the rest!

One chooses hastily, then off the porch he's flown,
Another chooses thoughtfully the prize he wants to own.
Each now has a treasure and it's safely packed away,
Now it's on to other houses, hunting brand new prey.

I close the door still smiling, I wink at my spouse,
Then, suddenly, I realize there are creatures in my house.
They sort of look familiar, in a cute kind of way,
In soft and pleading voices, I can hear them say—

Will you take us trick-or-treating? We really want to go.
It is dark enough now, you can see our flashlights glow.
Out the door they drag me, down the steps and past the gate,
Hurry up daddy, it's getting kind of late!

Snowfall

Down from the sky rained crystals of white,
Light, frothy things like feathers in flight.
White covered the ground and dusted the trees,
White clung to the window, blown there by the breeze.

Tiny, like lint balls, or dust bunnies under the bed,
Falling in torrents on the ground and my head.
Falling softly and slowly in a gently drifting quest,
Dreamily floating then finally coming to rest.

Flakes stick to flakes making a blanket of white,
Flakes keep on falling all through the night.
Accumulating deeply, first inches then feet,
Inundating everything in a cover complete.

Outside there's a world so pristine and untouched,
Total newness un-played-in, un-tromped-on, unclutched.
The serenity is broken as two anxious feet race,
Creating a wake in the snow that looks frozen in place.

Other feet follow, laughter rings through the air,
Snowballs go flying, children play without care.
Erected snowmen stand as sentinels outside snow-fort
walls.
Sleds create paths that look like frozen river falls.

I see the walls of an igloo, the kids haven't finish the rest,
A huge carved out snowball makes a tub or a nest.
I stare at a spot in the snow that the kids walk around,
I see they have made a snow angel there on the ground.

The children are playing with gusto and glee,
No flake looks untouched as far as I can see.
Night falls. In the warm house they shed their Eskimo
gear,
New snow is falling, filling the children with cheer.

Reflecting Christmas lights, the flakes glow brighter than
Mars,
Look out my window, daddy, I see falling stars!
Such wonder and awe in those admiring eyes,
As she watches the snowflakes filling the skies.

When the mountain caps lengthen and flow past their
toe,
When the valleys are filled with white wonder below,
When the roads are all slick and the car just won't go,
I'll never look out and see just plain snow!

Winter Fun

Down the slushy slope they came with squeals of delight
In a ship of plastic on a vast and foamy sea of white.
Cap tassels tossed and blown in an exhilarating breeze,
Sprinkled with ice and snow from an old winter freeze.

The valiant soldiers then led a charge upon the snow-
capped hill,
Slipping, sliding, falling down, stepping lightly to avoid a
spill.

Holding hands and toting sleds, treading carefully in the snow,
With a final effort, they crest the top and view the glory of all below.

Then to fly on winter wings, racing at break-neck speeds,
Carving trails down winter slopes where once stood summer weeds.
The sound of laughter mixed with the thrill of the run,
That's the taste of sledding, it's the best of winter fun.

A Day in the Mountains

We open the car door to the sweet smell of pine,
The cool mountain air feels simply divine.
We hear the soft gurgle of a meandering stream,
If this isn't heaven then it's only a dream.

Far from the angry clamor of city noise and life,
Far from the crowded corners and city streets of strife.
When the glare in the distance is 10 billion stars,
The brightest of all are Jupiter and Mars.

Small animals frolic in the lush meadows there,
The soft chirp of crickets can be heard on the air.
We're surrounded by the majesty of snow peaked
mountains,
And awed by the ever-flowing stream fountains.

Armed with a creel and our fisherman's poles,
We quietly seek out the best fishing holes.
With bait on our hooks, we all silently wish,
That our efforts will lead to catching some fish.

The day drifts away like a leaf on the stream,
Where a playful splash can bring a laugh or a scream.
Then a meal is cooked on a crackling fire,
S'mores for desert is what we desire.

When darkness arrives stories are told,
We play games with the flashlight if it's not too cold.
The safe in our tent we retire for the night,
For tomorrow it's back to the old city fight.

I Love the Way You Look at Me

I love the way you look at me,
With twinkling eyes aglow.
I love the radiance of your smile,
That tells me you really know.

I love the time you spend with me,
All cradled in my arms.
I love all the beauty that is you,
And all your womanly charms.

I love the little things you say,
To let me know you care.
I love the laughter in your voice,
And the secrets that we share.

I love the way you love our kids,
And all of your patient care.
I love how much they love you too,
And how you're always there.

To comfort, support, and teach and lift.
Your touch is an angel's caress,
Each day you give, the perfect gift.
There's no doubt, you are the best.

It's That Time of Year Again

I flinch as I hear the stark ringing bell,
I open my pack to that new paper smell.
I cringe at the squeal of chalk on the board.
Then stare out the window at a parked Ford.

I shudder to think that summer's now gone,
I picture brown patches and snow on the lawn.
I dream of hot days, and dips in the pool,
But, that's all next year, 'cuz I'm back in school.

Ode to Cookies and Milk

From a pool of white,
Where morsels swim,
And when sodden, flow freely from my cup.

The spoon draws a byte,
To a mustached grin,
Which eats and drinks the concoction up.

Don't Forget to Say I Love You

"I love you," he thought, and at the instant he thought it, she interrupted her slow and swaying stride towards the door to look at him. A knowing smile slowly spread across her face, and a twinkle lit her eyes. Her lips pucker then part, as she blew a kiss across the room. She took another step through the doorway, her eyes lingering on him for one last moment. Then she was gone. He recovered slightly and wondered, had he said it out loud? Or was it just coincidence that she turned at the very moment he had formulated the words he wanted to say? He would say it later, he wouldn't let another chance go by without telling her.

"I love you," he thought as he looked up from his work. She was at the table with the children. They were busy with homework. She was struggling to keep up with the questions and demands—"mom what do I have to do on this page?" "Will you give me my spelling words so I can practice for my test?" "Can you listen to me read now?…" She stopped and look down at him. Their eyes locked, and for an instant the noise dimmed, then stopped altogether. In spite of everything going on around them, for the instant, it was only the two of them. She smiled, "hi honey," she said. "Hello dear," he responded. Then time and space caught up with them. The world crashed in again and she was back to the kid's homework. He reluctantly returned to his work. I'll tell her when I'm done, he thought.

"I love you," he thought, as her car finished pulling out of the driveway. She was taking the older kids to clogging practice, the younger children were staying home with him. She took her car out of reverse and put it into drive. She turned her head, smiled and waved. He waved back. Then her car went forward and around the corner. Her presence drained from the house, as water drains form a cup with a hole in the bottom. "We're going to have fun," he says to the boys, but he looks at the place where her car had been just moments before and he knows he is going to miss her, even if it is only for a couple of hours.

"I love you," he thought, as an image of her at home passed through his mind. She had gone to visit a friend, he and the children had gone to the park. He was hoping she had returned, and was looking forward to seeing her. He pushed the garage door opener, and saw that her car was not in the garage. "Maybe if I go around the block again, she will be there when I get back," he thought."

"Dad, you missed our house," cried the kids. "It's back there!"

"I love you," he thought as she gently chided him. "I can't believe you still can't fold the clothes right. I have shown you how to fold shirts a dozen times over the last 14 years."

"I can't believe she puts up with me after all of that," he thought. "Maybe in another 14 years, I'll get it right," he says.

"I love you," he said, as they had finally gotten the kids to sleep and were at long-last laying down to rest. She rolled towards him and pressed her body close to his. She placed her face right next to his, "I love you too," she said. She kissed him tenderly, then rolled back. Soon her even breathing let him know that she was asleep. Somehow, her presence filled him with warmth and comfort. It was knowing she was there that gave him peace and guarded his dreams at night. Even the occasional cough from the children, and the sound of rain and wind outside would not interrupt his slumber tonight. "Of course, she loves me too," were his last thoughts as he drifted off to sleep.

The End

If you enjoyed this volume of Life's Poetry, please leave a review on Amazon. Thank you.

You can review the book here:
http://amzn.to/1QTnDnl

Dean Giles

Appendix

Thank you for reading the book!

If you enjoyed these short stories, please leave a Review.

https://www.amazon.com/review/create-review?ie=UTF8&asin=B014N2E9CU.

Reviews help so much! Thank you in advance.

Dean R. Giles

About the Author

Dean R. Giles has been an avid reader his entire life. He preferred reading to doing homework through a lot of his school years. Writing became part of his work through every job that he had. He has contributed to numerous technical manuals, information products, and detailed reports over the years. Story telling was a favorite activity with his children over a number of years.

Writing books became a natural extension of various interests. He began studying writing in the late 2000s and began publishing books in 2011.

If you have any feedback, questions, or just want to drop me a note, you can send an email to dean@austinsgift.com .

Find out about my upcoming Fantasy novel at Austinsgift.com/magic.

Other Books by This Author:

About Writing

How to Steal Like an Author:
http://www.amazon.com/dp/B00NVN99FK
Discover Book Ideas:
http://www.amazon.com/dp/B00IODSNVI
Write On
http://www.amazon.com/dp/B00O9LIBMK

Not About Writing

Dragons Restored
http://www.amazon.com/dp/B014N2E9CU
Life's Poetry
http://www.amazon.com/dp/B00UU0UQ2C
The Snow Birthday
http://www.amazon.com/dp/B00BWAP6SS
Summer Time Fun
http://www.amazon.com/dp/B00DZVYG4W
Keyword Planner
http://www.amazon.com/dp/B00E45ADKE

Connect with me

Email: dean@autstinsgift.com
Blog: http://austinsgift.com
Facebook:
https://www.facebook.com/DragonsRestored/
 Sign up for my email list:
http://austinsgift.com/writing